D0993860

Report Writing
in a week

KATHARINE HERITAGE

Hodder & Stoughton

A MEMBER OF THE HODDER HEADLINE GROUP

Orders: please contact Bookpoint Ltd, 130 Milton Park, Abingdon, Oxon OX14 4SB. Telephone: (44) 01235 827720, Fax: (44) 01235 400454. Lines are open from 9.00 - 6.00, Monday to Saturday, with a 24 hour message answering service. Email address: orders@bookpoint.co.uk

British Library Cataloguing in Publication Data
A catalogue record for this title is available from The British Library

ISBN 0 340 849568

First published 1997
Impression number   10   9   8   7   6   5   4   3   2   1
Year   2007 2006 2005 2004 2003

Cover image: Image Bank/Getty Images

Typeset by SX Composing DTP, Rayleigh, Essex
Printed in Great Britain for Hodder & Stoughton Educational, a division of Hodder Headline Plc, 338 Euston Road, London NW1 3BH by Cox & Wyman Ltd, Reading, Berkshire.

The leading organisation for professional management

As the champion of management, the Chartered Management Institute shapes and supports the managers of tomorrow. By sharing intelligent insights and setting standards in management development, the Institute helps to deliver results in a dynamic world.

Setting and raising standards

The Institute is a nationally accredited organisation, responsible for setting standards in management and recognising excellence through the award of professional qualifications.

Encouraging development, improving performance

The Institute has a vast range of development programmes, qualifications, information resources and career guidance to help managers and their organisations meet new challenges in a fast-changing environment.

Shaping opinion

With in-depth research and regular policy surveys of its 91,000 individual members and 520 corporate members, the Chartered Management Institute has a deep understanding of the key issues. Its view is informed, intelligent and respected.

For more information call 01536 204222 or visit www.managers.org.uk

C O N T E N T S

Introduction		5
Sunday	Setting the objective	7
Monday	Researching and organising information	17
Tuesday	Structuring the report	28
Wednesday	Writing in a clear style	40
Thursday	Using correct English	55
Friday	Adding the finishing touches	69
Saturday	Checklist of key points	83

You will find reports in the out-trays of managers everywhere: reports to the board, monthly reports, research reports and scores of other types of reports. Even a memo is often simply a short form of report.

Every manager has to write reports occasionally, and most have to write them frequently. Reports are a standard management tool without which it would be impossible to function effectively.

Despite this, most managers are expected to write reports without any training whatsoever. But the difference between a good report and a bad report can be the difference between achieving your objective and failing to achieve it. It can be the difference between impressing your superiors and disappointing them.

A bad report may contain all the facts, but presentation – in terms of structure, language and layout – is often the clinching factor.

The basic guidelines for report writing are the same for everything, from hefty research reports to inter-departmental memos. This book looks at the key stages of report writing, from the moment you receive the brief until the final document is ready to send off to the person for whom it was written. These stages are:

- Setting the objective

- Researching and organising the information

- Structuring the report

- Writing in a clear style

- Using correct English

- Adding the finishing touches

Setting the objective

Today we look at the first stage of report writing: setting the objective. This covers:

- Why you need an objective
- How to set the objective
- Making the objective specific
- Agreeing the objective

The first thing to do when you are asked to produce a report is to set a clear objective for it. Quite apart from anything else, this will make you focus clearly and do some hard thinking right at the start of the process. And a few minutes of structured thinking now can save you hours of work later.

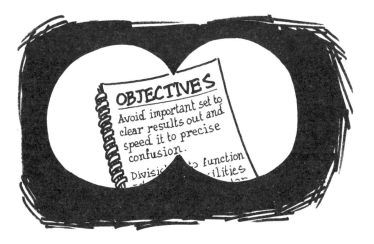

The objective you need will take the form of a single sentence which expresses clearly what you intend the report to achieve. We'll look at how to set this objective shortly, but first let's establish why it's so important to go through this process.

Why you need an objective

Many people think that setting an objective before you start is a waste of time. After all, you must know what the report is supposed to be about, mustn't you? It can seem particularly pointless when the report is a regular one, such as a monthly management report. But in fact, a clearly written objective has a number of important benefits:

- It helps you decide what information to include or leave out
- It helps you pitch the report appropriately for the reader
- It makes it easier to write the report

Deciding what to include or leave out
A clear objective gives you a touchstone against which you can measure any available information, and decide whether it should be included or not. If you don't have a clear objective, you can often spend ages researching all the information you could possibly need, only to find later that you didn't need half of it after all. One of the functions of a good objective is to ensure that you don't waste time at the research stage of the process.

Pitching the report appropriately for the reader
The objective should always state exactly who the intended readers are. This helps you to focus on making sure that

you include the information they want, expressed in the way they want it.

Examples

Suppose you're writing a report reviewing the effectiveness of your new computer networking system after it's been up and running for six months. If the report is for the board of directors, they will probably want to know about the system's general teething problems and its effect on productivity – they are not likely to understand highly technical language. If the report is for your technical department, however, they are likely to want far more detail about the actual operation of the system, and in this case you can include detailed technical language.

To give you another example, a report on the launch of a new product would need a different emphasis if it were written for the Marketing Director from the emphasis which the Finance Director would want. The Marketing Director would want more detail about customer response, while the Finance Director would have a special interest in costings.

Making it easier to write the report
When you come to write and structure the report, you'll find it's a much quicker process if you're already clear in your own mind exactly what you're trying to achieve. You may think you know this already, but once you've tried writing a report with a clear objective already set, you'll discover just how much easier it becomes.

How to set the objective

The first thing to do when you come to set the objective is to be clear about the rough idea behind the report. You will most likely know this already. For example, you may be reporting on the effectiveness of your recent exhibition attendancies, or feeding back the results of your study into how best to reallocate the offices on the fourth floor. Or you may simply be giving a monthly update on your department's activities.

So far, so good. But these objectives are too fuzzy to be really useful. In order to make your objective clearer, you need to ask yourself a few questions. These questions are all geared to the point of view of your readers; after all, you're writing the report for them, not for yourself. If you don't keep your readers constantly in mind, you can end up with a report full of pertinent information which imparts nothing useful to them at all.

Thinking about all these things, for every report you write, is a vital step in setting the objective. If you are writing a report for the sales department about new products in development, for example, your readers will want the information so that they can let customers know what products are in the pipeline, and perhaps get customer feedback to help fine tune the products. They will therefore want to know about the benefits to customers of the new products; they won't need to know which suppliers you're planning to use. And you can refer to existing products, or draw comparisons with them, confident that the sales people need no explanations – they know as much as anyone about your current product range.

Once you have thought through the answers to all these questions, you should be able to put together a concise sentence that explains your objective simply and clearly.

How about: *To update the sales department on forthcoming products?* Well, that's a good start, but armed with the answers to the previous questions, you should be able to make your objective a lot more specific. And the more specific it is, the more useful it will be as a touchstone against which to assess your report.

Making the objective specific

Using an objective is a bit like using a route map. If you're setting out to drive from Cardiff to Aberdeen, you don't tend to get in the car and drive off blindly. You look at a map and decide in advance roughly which route to take. Before you start the engine you'll know you're going to Bristol, then heading north as far as Glasgow, and then driving cross-country up to Aberdeen.

Instead of striking out randomly – and perhaps ending up calling at Exeter and Hull on your way to Aberdeen – you work out the route that fits your requirements most precisely. In this case your requirements may be speed, comfort and low fuel costs.

An objective provides you with the same outline route map. Of course, the requirements may be different. So you establish what they are in advance, and build them into your objective. And you identify your requirements from the answers to the questions we asked earlier.

Let's go back to the objective:

> To update the sales department on
> forthcoming products

That's all very well, but it's rather a broad brief. It could include giving them production costings, detailed specifications that the customers don't understand, and all sorts of other information.

Let's narrow it down a bit:

> To update the sales department on information for
> customers about forthcoming products

That's much better. That's saved having to research all that other stuff that we didn't actually need – product specifications and so on. But it could still be just a little bit clearer. The sales department especially want to know the benefits, or selling points, of the new products. That's very important, and we haven't really made it clear in the objective.

We'll try again, making it even more specific this time:

> To update the sales department on information for customers about forthcoming products, focusing particularly on the benefits to customers

Now we have a really clear objective that leaves us in no doubt as to where the emphasis of the report should be. And we can measure any piece of information against it to assess whether it should be included or not.

Agreeing the objective

There's one more huge advantage to setting a clear objective. You can go back to the person who asked for the report and ask them to have a look at the objective and make sure they agree with it.

Suppose your boss asks for a written report on the new product range you launched a couple of months ago. So you talk to the sales team about the responses from customers, and collect the latest sales figures. After days of hard work, you take your report back to your boss who looks at it and says, 'No, no, no. I don't want that sort of information. I want to know whether we're getting maintenance problems and faults, whether production and stock levels are running efficiently, how well our suppliers are operating . . . that sort of thing'.

Sounds familiar? It happens to most of us sooner or later – unless we put a specific objective in writing before we start. If you'd taken your objective to the boss as soon as you'd written it, you could have had exactly the same conversation, but you'd have wasted only minutes instead of days.

Summary

Today we looked at the crucial starting point for writing any report: the objective.

We established *why* we need an objective; we looked at the guidelines for setting the objective; and we established how to make the objective specific – how to draw up the route map. We've also seen how setting a clear objective from the start can help you to make certain that you and your boss – or whoever asked for the report – are both thinking along the same lines.

There's one more point worth making about setting objectives. Once you've got into the habit of doing it when you write reports, you'll find it's an invaluable skill for all sorts of other management projects as well. You'll derive all the same benefits from setting objectives for giving presentations, organising exhibitions, commissioning agencies, planning projects and numerous other management skills.

Researching and organising information

Today we look at how to gather together the information you need to write the report, and how to organise it logically. There are four steps in this process:

- Decide what information you need
- Collect the material
- Collate the information
- Sort it into groups

If the report you're writing is at all sizeable, this stage of the process can be pretty daunting. So far you've written one line – your objective – and you've still got everything else to do. However, the objective will prove extremely useful, as you'll soon see, and by the end of this stage you should be feeling far happier about the task. It will all come together during this stage.

Decide what information you need

You'll have to sit down and think this through, either on your own or with other people, whichever seems the most useful. It often helps to ask the person you are writing the report for to tell you if there are specific areas they want covered.

And already, your written objective should prove useful. Have a look at it and see what it tells you. To begin with, you want a list of general topics that you feel you should cover. Our objective from yesterday was:

> To update the sales department on information for customers about forthcoming products, focusing particularly on the benefits to customers

Now you can draw up a list of general areas to cover that looks something like this:

- Description of products
- Comparisons with competitors' products
- Key benefits to customers
- Sales support
- Brochures/literature
- Supplementary information

At this stage, it doesn't matter what order you list these in; you're just getting them down on paper. Brainstorm everything you might want to include, and check it against the objective to make sure it's appropriate for your report.

Once you've done this, you can start to list individual topics under each of these headings. For example, under supplementary information you might include:

- Product launch dates
- Prices
- Delivery times
- Guarantees

You can draw up this list and sublists any way you like. These are your own notes; there are no rules. You might want to start a fresh sheet of paper for each one, or you may prefer to use a form of mind mapping, if you like to work that way.

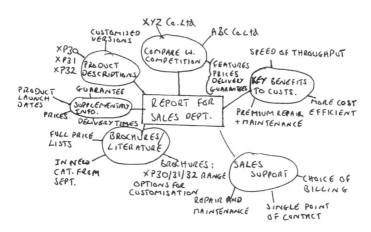

This is an important process to go through, albeit briefly, even with a regular report. Suppose you put together a monthly management report and you always use the same headings. If something happens that has never occurred before, it may not fit into any of your headings, and could be forgotten altogether. Using this approach forces your thinking to be led by the facts, rather than allowing you to switch to auto-pilot when it comes to routine reports.

Collect the material

Now you have your list, you can go through it again and decide where is the best place to look for each piece of information you've decided that you need. You might want to use copies of reports produced by other departments, or minutes of meetings. Or you might want to get hold of information about competitors' products – their brochures and price lists and so on.

For some reports, you might need to collect very little information, while others may require a great deal. If you were writing a report on the current state of the market you're involved in, you might need lots of material from outside your own organisation, such as articles in the trade press, or lists of competitors.

If you're putting together a report with recommendations – perhaps outlining the options for improving and renovating your premises and then recommending the most suitable one to the board of directors – you'll need all sorts of costings and projections.

In general, there are three sources you can go to for information:

- Material from inside your organisation
- Publicly available material
- Information you get from talking to people

We'll have a look at each of these three in a bit more detail.

Material from inside the organisation
You'll often find that most of the information you want to include in your report already exists in your organisation;

it's just a matter of digging it out. Have a look at:

- Your own sales literature
- Internal newsletters or magazines
- Customer newsletters or magazines
- Regular reports, including monthly or quarterly figures
- Minutes of meetings
- Reports and proposals prepared by other departments

Publicly available material

Once you've collected everything you can internally, have a look at all the sources of information from outside the organisation:

- Books and booklets on relevant aspects of the subject
- Business and trade directories (in any main library)
- Directories of market research reports (also in the library)
- Newspapers, magazines and trade press
- Research findings and statistics produced by trade associations
- Publications and reports from government departments (listed by the Central Statistical Office)
- Competitors' brochures, catalogues, annual reports and sales literature

Talking to people

This information may come from inside or outside your organisation; either way, it's surprising how much

information you can get just from phoning someone up or
going to see them. Talk to the following:

- Customers – survey them on the phone or face-to-
  face
- Experts, both in the company and outside it – get
  specialist information from them
- Suppliers – ask them for costings, availability of
  materials and so on

Copyright

If you reproduce anyone else's material in your report you
are in breach of copyright (apart from short, attributed
quotes); even if the report is for internal distribution only.
The copyright is in the words only, however. You're safe if
you take the meaning but rewrite it using your own words.
Alternatively, contact the author or copyright owner and
ask their permission to use the material (and get their
agreement in writing).

Collate the information

So you've gathered together all your books and brochures, reports and interview notes. The next stage may seem slightly laborious – especially if you have a lot of material – but it's more than worth it. Collating the material now will save you masses of time later on, and it will help you to get to know your material really well, even at this early stage.

Start by putting all your research material in a pile on one side of the desk. Now work through it, writing down each main point that you want to incorporate into the report on a separate piece of paper. As you go through, the pile of research material dwindles, and you find a collection of slips of paper accumulating on your desk.

This doesn't actually take as long as you might think. You don't need to write down the details, just the main points. So you might have a collection of competitors' price lists, and a corresponding slip of paper that says 'comparison between our prices and our competitors' prices'.

It's also a good idea to make a note on the slip of paper telling yourself where this information comes from, so you can lay your hands on it easily when you come to use it.

This stage can be speeded up if you make notes on a word processor, since you just print everything out and then cut up the paper so that each main point is on a separate slip.

Once you've been through all your material, you'll have dozens of scraps of paper on your desk. Between them, these scraps hold all the information you need for your report. It's all down on paper which means you don't have to hold any of the information in your head.

Regular reports
If you are producing a regular report, you can jot down notes on slips of paper, or small index cards, all the time. If you do this for, say, a monthly departmental report, it makes the job of writing it really quick. When the time comes to produce the report, you just pull out all your bits of paper from your drawer or box, and there's your information, ready-made.

Sort the information into groups

You now have all the information you need to write your report. What's more, you don't have to wade through piles of books and reports to review it – all the important points are on manageable pieces of paper. The next stage is to organise them.

This is where having separate pieces of paper is so useful. What you do now is to sort them into groups, and since they are all separate you can move each piece of paper around until you feel it is in the most sensible group.

You may well find that you organise this information into groups that correspond to the main headings on your original list – the one you drew up when you were deciding what information you needed to collect. These were:

- Description of products
- Comparisons with competitors' products
- Key benefits to customers
- Sales support
- Brochures/literature
- Supplementary information

You may find that some other kind of grouping seems more logical now that you've got the information together. Or perhaps it looks as though it would help to split one of these sections into two, or merge two sections together. This is fine – just do whatever seems logical.

It's difficult to give a clear idea of the number of groups you want, because reports can vary so much in scope and length. But generally speaking, you're probably looking for between about four and a dozen groups.

At this stage, you're not yet grouping the information into the final structure for the report. You needn't worry about that yet. You're just turning a random collection of notes into a few key groups of notes.

This process will help you to focus on your subject and, as you organise your slips of paper, you'll find your mind becomes more organised as well. But this process has two other key benefits:

1 Most of the material will probably stay in the same groups when it comes to structuring the report (whatever order the groups end up in), so you're saving yourself work later on
2 As you go through each piece of paper deciding which group to put it in, you can check it against

your objective just to make sure that it really does belong in the report. It also means you can make sure you don't duplicate information

Summary

By the end of this stage you have all the information you are going to need for your report, and you have condensed it onto pieces of paper which are arranged in logical groupings. You have reached this point by:

- Thinking through what information you need, and listing topics to include
- Collecting the information from inside and outside the organisation, and from talking to people
- Collating the information by writing the main points down on pieces of paper
- Organising the pieces of paper into logical groupings

Most people start to feel a lot happier at this stage. The research work is all done, and everything is down in writing so you no longer have to hold any information in your head. Tomorrow, we look at how you can turn these groups of paper notes into a clear and logical structure for your report.

Structuring the report

Today, we look at the final stage of preparation: structuring the report. There are two different types of report, which each call for a different structure:

- Research reports
- Information-only reports

Research reports are those where you investigate a subject and then make a report about your findings. You might be researching your competitors' activities, or looking at options for a new computer system. Sometimes, research reports can include recommendations; for example reporting on products in development and recommending which to go ahead with first.

Information-only reports simply pass on information – as the term implies. These include memos, updates and regular budget reports, management reports and so on.

We now look at how to structure each of these types of report.

Research reports

Research reports can be terribly important. For one thing, these reports often form the basis for decisions on which new products to launch, whether to open up another branch, how to invest the company's reserves or whether to enter a new market.

But these reports can also be crucial from a personal point of view. Many people are first noticed by senior management because of a research report, and they can be important stepping stones in your career.

Well put together, a research report shows that you have a talent for clear, logical, ordered and objective thinking – important skills in management. Poorly structured reports, however, give precisely the opposite impression; even if all the relevant facts are buried in them somewhere. So it's particularly important to learn how to structure this kind of report clearly.

If you did chemistry or physics at school, you may remember that there was a standard format for writing up all those experiments involving Bunsen burners and pipettes. In case it wasn't etched into your brain as deeply as your science teacher would have wished, this is how it went:

- Aim
- Method
- Results
- Conclusion

A scientific experiment is a form of research, of course, and the write-up afterwards is a report on that research. So it should be no surprise to learn that your science teacher was right. This is exactly the way to write a research report: aim, method, results, conclusion.

Aim

You may remember that the aim of those science experiments always had to be expressed in a single sentence, and the same goes for your research report. You have, of course, already composed your sentence: your objective that you worked out right at the start.

For an information report you would work this out and then keep it to yourself. But for a research report, it is usually helpful for the reader if you actually state your objective at the very beginning of your report. You can head it 'aim' or 'objective' or whatever you like.

Example

The aim of this research was to ascertain whether
reducing our delivery times to less than 72 hours
would appeal to customers, improve customer
satisfaction and be cost-effective.

Method

The method section of your report explains how you
established the answers to these questions. In the scientific
experiments your 'method' would have read, for example:
*We took 2mg copper sulphate and dissolved it at room
temperature in 6ml of hydrochloric acid, by stirring it with a
glass rod*

For a research report, you want to outline the methods you
used. This should be comprehensive but not detailed; for
example you might want to say that you used business
directories, but don't give a detailed bibliography. Or you
could mention that you ran a survey of your suppliers, but
don't list all the questions on it. If you wish, these sorts of
details can be added later on in the report – in the
appendices. The type of research methods you want to list
here would include:

- Written sources of material (briefly – not a detailed
  bibliography)
- Any interviews you conducted
- Any written surveys you carried out
- Any tests you conducted

Here's an example of how the 'method' section of your report might read:

Example

We designed a customer survey card (see appendix) which we distributed to all customers nationwide with every delivery. This card was designed to measure customer satisfaction.

After running this scheme for a month, to establish normal satisfaction levels, we piloted a scheme in our East Anglia region in which we offered customers delivery within 24 hours. We then monitored whether this change in service affected the level of customer satisfaction measured by the survey cards.

At the same time, we monitored how many customers opted for faster delivery, and assessed the cost of this. We also noted whether these customers were more likely than others to show a higher level of satisfaction.

"We held each of our customers over a Bunsen burner flame and asked if they were happy with the service they were getting."

Results

In this section of the report, you can write everything that you discovered from your research. It is likely to make up by far the largest part of your report. However, you should only present the facts – this is not the place to draw conclusions.

DON'T EXPECT ME TO HAVE AN OPINION UNTIL PAGE 7

You should present all the important data here, but don't get bogged down in unnecessary detail; you can save that for the appendix. The word 'unnecessary' is important here. After all, sometimes detail is necessary. If you're writing a complex technical report for engineers who not only understand but also need to know the minutiae, you should include most of the details here.

But if the detail is unlikely to concern your readers, leave it for the appendix where it will simply support your main findings for the benefit of those who want extra information.

Having said that, you can include any charts, graphs and diagrams in this section that are important to the main thrust of the report. Here's an example of how your 'results' section might look:

Example

In the first part of the research, we established that the average satisfaction rating nationally under the 'delivery' section of the survey card was 72%. The variation on this was within 4% either way, and the average for East Anglia was 73% satisfaction. (See appendix for full results by region.)

When we introduced the 24-hour delivery pilot scheme, the satisfaction rating in East Anglia rose to 84%. The average for the remainder of the country remained the same as before.

Costs

We found that during the four-week trial period, 17% of our customers took up the option of faster delivery. Using our normal courier service, the extra cost for delivering within 24 hours instead of 72 hours is £3.28 per item. However, if we introduced this service across the country the discount would reduce this cost to £2.47.

The satisfaction rating increased among East Anglia customers who didn't use the fast delivery option, as well as those who did. However, it increased more among those customers who did opt for the 24-hour service (see graph).

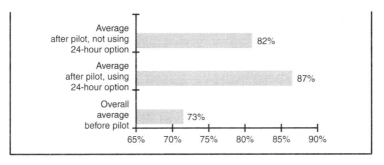

Conclusion

The conclusion, which may be anything from a paragraph to a page or so in length, should refer back to the original objective or 'aim', just as it always did in those school science experiments. Read through your original objective before you decide precisely what to say in your conclusion, to keep your mind well focused on it.

This is your opportunity – at last – to express the opinion you've been bottling up until now. Do you think you should offer a 24-hour delivery service throughout the country? Now's your chance to say what you think.

Example

It seems that customer satisfaction increases as a result of being offered a faster delivery service. Even those customers who did not want to use the fast delivery showed a higher level of satisfaction simply because they had been offered the choice.

Since a relatively small percentage of customers actually took up the 24-hour delivery option, the cost implications would be lower than feared.

The additional cost seems a relatively small price to pay for a significant increase in satisfaction among all customers, not only those who use the 24-hour service.

I would conclude from this research that we should introduce the 24-hour delivery option nationwide.

Information-only reports

This type of report is much easier to structure. In fact, you'll be pleased to know that if you're writing an information-only report, you've pretty well structured it already.

As you probably know from experience, there is no rigid structure that you can follow for this kind of report. The important thing is simply to avoid a messy and illogical structure.

Just to recap, when you sit down to structure the report, you have several piles of paper slips in front of you, sorted into groups. All you have to do now is to put those groups into a sensible order. That's the most helpful thing you can do to make the report clear for your readers.

Sometimes there is a fairly logical way to order these groups, for example:

- In date order
- By department
- In order of importance
- By turnover
- By size (for customers, say)
- By geographical location (for sales areas, for instance)
- In an existing order that the reader knows (such as products in the catalogue)

This is not an exhaustive list; just a few ideas. Once you have put the groups in order you can organise the information – or slips of paper – within each group in the same way.

Occasionally you'll find that there simply isn't any logical order for the groups at all. Or perhaps the first three or four could go in order of importance but after that each group is of equal importance. If there isn't a logical order, you obviously can't use one, so don't worry. Sometimes it really doesn't make any difference what order the groups go in.

Just remember the aim of the exercise. You want to do everything you can to help your readers to:

- Follow the information and take it in as easily as possible

- Understand it
- Be able to go back later and find any information quickly if they want to recap

So long as you're achieving that, you've structured your report as well as you could.

Summary

Today we looked at the two different types of report you could be asked to write, and the best way to structure each one. The two basic types are research reports and information-only reports, and these are the best structures for each:

Structuring research reports

- Aim
- Method
- Results
- Conclusion

Structuring information-only reports

- Use the groups you have already organised the information into
- Where possible, put these groups into a logical sequence
- Put the information within each group into a logical sequence

The important thing to remember is that you are doing everything you can to make it as easy as possible for the reader to follow and understand the report. If you achieve that aim, you've structured your report well.

Now you've completed the preparation stages of writing your report: setting the objective, researching, organising the information and structuring. You've actually done most of the hard work already. Tomorrow, it's time to get the pen out or turn on the word processor, and start writing.

Writing in a clear style

Today we look at how to write clear English. This is a separate thing from how to use the language accurately – grammar and so on – which we look at tomorrow. The topics we'll cover today include:

- Overall style
- Phrasing
- Words

The real secret of good writing style, the attitude you should approach any writing with, is to write pretty much as you speak. Of course you need to avoid the extremes of slang, but material is always harder to read when it is written in stilted language that the reader is unfamiliar with.

Many of us find it easy to talk clearly, and express arguments in a well-structured way. But when we come to transfer these techniques onto paper we have a sudden need to impress with long words and complicated sentences. This is dangerous in a report because it gets in the way of the message, and the report loses clarity and effect.

Overall style

Remember who you're writing the report for: the reader, not yourself. So you need to adapt your own natural style to suit the reader. In many cases, this may require little or no change. But you need to think about it because sometimes your readers aren't quite the same as you.

For example, suppose you're writing a report for your board of directors, who happen to be predominantly over 55 and perhaps rather stuffy. Modern rules of English (as we'll see in the next chapter) allow you to use dashes for parenthesis – like this – which was never considered proper in traditional English grammar.

If your board of directors were educated at grammar schools and public schools before about 1960, they probably have old fashioned attitudes to English usage. So, if you want their approval of your report, it's as well to stick to *their* idea of what constitutes good English.

You shouldn't need to change your style completely; simply adapt it to accommodate the readers' likely style. This principle doesn't apply only to older readers. You may have to adapt your use of language for other groups as well. Here are a few examples:

- People with a more traditional style of English than yours
- People whose style is more modern than yours
- People for whom English is not the first language
- People with reading difficulties (such as dyslexia)

Use ordinary English

Unless your readers fall into one of the previous categories, such as the very traditional type, use idiomatic, everyday English. This doesn't mean slang, however. So instead of using a formal word or phrase like 'female persons' you should say 'women' – but not 'girls' or 'birds'.

Elision

It's also more natural to elide certain words (or run them together). So you could write, for example, 'isn't' rather than 'is not', and 'we'll' rather than 'we will'. This is easier for people to read, since it's the way we speak (although it's also an example of a more modern style to avoid with very old-fashioned readers).

Avoid stilted language

For some reason, people are often prone to use particular words and phrases in reports that no one uses in real life. The effect is to make the report read like a police statement, full of 'persons proceeding in vehicles' instead of 'people driving cars'. Here are some of the more commonly used expressions:

Expression	Alternative
in respect of	about
at this moment in time	now
in the event of	if
terminate	stop, or end
ascertain	find out
in consequence	so

This is a matter of style rather than individual words because you don't need to learn each one of these (and there are plenty more). All you need to do is learn to adopt the general approach of writing as you speak, rather than slipping into stilted language.

Use 'I' and 'you'

When you speak to someone you refer to yourself as 'I' and to them as 'you'. Do this when you write as well. Not only is it easier to read, but it's also far friendlier. If you're writing on behalf of your department, for instance, you can say 'we' rather than 'I'. It's surprising how many people will write, *The recommendation of this report is for the purchase of . . .* , when they could say, *We recommend you buy . . .*

Be politically correct

Regardless of your own views on this subject (and of course, it's not your views but those of your readers' that matter), any lack of political correctness these days appears out of touch and old-fashioned. Many readers may not be bothered by any racism, ageism or sexism you display, but will think to themselves 'Goodness! I didn't think anyone still used such out-of-date language!' So whatever your personal view, avoid '-isms' of all sorts.

Avoid sexist language

Many people find it particularly difficult to write in non-sexist language. This is understandable since most of us grew up using 'he' to mean 'he or she'. However, there are several techniques for avoiding sexist language very easily:

1 Put the sentence into the plural. Instead of saying, *Each employee should enrol on a course to learn to use his laptop PC effectively,* you can say, *All employees should enrol on a course to learn to use their laptop PCs effectively.*

2 Use the second person ('you' or 'your'). Try saying *You can easily learn to use a laptop PC.* This not only gets round the problem, but also has a far friendlier feel to it.

3 Use 'they'. It's now considered acceptable to use the pronoun 'they' as a singular. So you can say *Even the most non-technically minded person can use a laptop PC if they put their mind to it.*

4 Alternate examples. If you're using examples, for instance types of customers or employees, you might want to identify their gender to make them sound more human. You can always vary the gender in this case. For example: *All sorts of employees come to us with time-keeping problems. The woman who can't quite make the last train if she leaves after 5 o'clock; the man who has to drop the kids at school on his way to work...* and so on.

5 Use 'he or she' or 'he/she'. This is the least satisfactory solution since it draws attention to itself, and can be intrusive. However, it is far better than using sexist language, so use it if you're really stuck for an alternative technique.

Use examples and analogies

When you talk to people face-to-face, they can stop you if they don't understand something, and ask you to go over it again. But if they're reading a report, they don't have that opportunity, so you have to make extra sure that you explain everything as well as you possibly can. And the two most useful tools for doing that are examples and analogies.

Sometimes you may think something is more obvious than it really is to other people. If you're in any doubt at all, give examples. It's never a bad thing, and it's often essential. Earlier on, we looked at how to avoid stilted language. If you hadn't had a few examples of stilted expressions to look at, you might not have found the point nearly so clear to follow.

Analogies can be invaluable for explaining complicated ideas. They usually start 'it's a bit like . . .' or 'it's as if . . .'. Suppose you want to explain the structure of an organisation. You'd be using an analogy if you said *It's rather like a tree. At the roots, holding everything in place, are the back office workers. Above the ground are the main trunks, or divisions, with smaller branches, or departments, attached to each one . . .* and so on.

THE WAY PEOPLE IN THIS DEPARTMENT FEEL ABOUT THE MANAGEMENT IS A BIT LIKE THE WAY A SMALL ZOO ANIMAL FEELS WHEN THE KEEPER FORGETS TO GIVE IT LUNCH FOR THE THIRD DAY RUNNING...

Phrasing

Once you've got the general style right, you're well on your way to producing clearly written reports. But it's still important that you use the right phrases and words within that style. We'll deal with the words in a minute, but first let's look at the phrases and sentences.

Use short sentences and short paragraphs

There are researchers who have spent months devising scales of readability, telling you how easy or difficult it is for people to read what you've written. Your word processing program may be able to give you a readability rating for what you've just written.

But without getting bogged down in detail, there are certain things that all these scales take into account. And among the most important are length of paragraph and length of sentence.

Paragraphs

If you open up a book or a report that has few or no paragraph breaks, you will almost certainly catch some part of your brain thinking 'Oh, no . . .'. It looks like so much to wade through. Not only that, but paragraphs help you to structure what you're saying, and without them it's much harder for the readers to identify the structure of what they are being asked to take in.

You should start a new paragraph every time you start a new thought. It can be bitty for your readers if you start a new paragraph with every sentence, but it is still better than having no paragraph breaks at all. At the very least, you should make sure that, if you're using standard A4 width paper, your paragraphs are wider than they are deep.

Sentences

Long sentences are tough to read. Your style would seem very monotonous if all the sentences were the same length, so it's best to go for variety. This also makes your writing more interesting and adds texture to it. However, you should aim to average about 20 words to a sentence, and you should rarely exceed 35. If you go over 40 words, you really ought to be able to shorten the sentence or break it down into two or more sentences.

Example

Here's an example of a long sentence, followed by a suggestion for shortening it.

In the event that two or more members of staff from the department are absent from work at the same time, it will become necessary for one or more of the remaining members of staff to provide cover to ensure that essential functions are still carried out until such time as the absent members of staff have returned to work.

There's always more than one way to shorten a sentence, but here's an example. You'll notice that as the sentence gets shorter, it becomes clearer.

If two or more people are away from the department at once, someone else should cover essential tasks until they get back.

Don't use jargon
Jargon can seem hard to define, but essentially it's specialised language that relates to a particular subject. We all use some jargon which, to us, has become everyday language. It's only jargon to other people. 'MS/DOS' is jargon to people who don't use computers.

Jargon exists because it's a really useful shorthand between people who are in the know. If you're quite certain that all your readers fall into this category, go ahead and use it. But you need to be clear about which of the words that you use every day are jargon to other people. Don't use them if there's any danger that your readers won't understand. Find an alternative word or phrase – the one your readers would use.

It can occasionally happen that you really can't avoid jargon, particularly in technical reports. If this is the case, and your readers may not understand it, the solution is to include a glossary (we look at glossaries on Friday).

Don't use clichés

Some expressions have become so hackneyed that they are effectively meaningless. Readers are so used to seeing the particular phrase that their brains no longer take it in. The business world, unfortunately, is plagued by these expressions. To give you a few examples:

- Meeting customer needs
- A wide range of products and services
- High quality products

These are all expressions that we've all seen too often to take them in properly any more. If they still mean anything at all, they've certainly lost all impact.

The last example is a good one. We hear so often about 'high quality products' that we no longer believe the phrase. Everyone says that about their products.

So how do you get round using these clichés? The answer is very simple, and carries far more weight than the clichés ever did, even when they were first coined. You quote hard facts.

So instead of saying *This product meets customer needs,* you say *Over the last two years, our surveys show that customer satisfaction is consistently above 97% on this product.* Or perhaps *Over 85% of our customers buy from us again within six months.*

You can describe your *high quality products* by saying, *Our products last an average of 12 years before needing to be replaced,* or, *In last year's industry survey our products performed better than any of our competitors'.*

Words

These are the final aspect of style that you need to consider. Again, there aren't right and wrong words to use, just general approaches to choosing your words. So once you've grasped the principle, you should find it very easy to choose the best words for your reports. There are just a few simple guidelines to follow.

Use short words when you can

Short words are far easier to read and help your writing to flow. A few long words are necessary, and used sparingly they add variety to your report. But why say 'vehicle' when you can say 'car'?

Long words your readers recognise readily are better than ones they are unfamiliar with. It's not so much of a sin to write 'encyclopedia' as it is to write 'recherché', even though 'encyclopedia' has more letters in it.

Use active rather than passive verbs

This means making the subject of the sentence do something, rather than have something done to it. *The dog chased the cat* is active, but *the cat was chased by the dog* is passive. Active verbs make writing more dynamic and readable. Having established the importance of examples a few pages back, you'd better have another one: *A percentage of staff pensions will be paid by the company* is passive. The active version would be *The company will pay a percentage of staff pensions.*

There are times when you need to use passive verbs, but since they slow the reader down limit yourself to about one every four or five sentences at the most. Here are some examples of when you may want or need to use passive verbs:

- When the subject (the person or thing *doing* the verb) is unknown or irrelevant: *The building was painted blue.*
- When you want the emphasis on the object of the sentence (the person or thing who something is

being done to): *The cars at the far end of the car park are the ones that are most often broken into*
- When you want to fudge the issue: *A mistake was made with this order.* (Fudging isn't a good idea in reports but, if you're going to do it, you'll find that passive verbs are a great help)

Use concrete rather than abstract nouns

A 'communication tool' is an abstract idea; a 'telephone' is a concrete one. Concrete nouns give readers a visual picture in their minds, which makes it far easier to take in the idea that goes with it.

Abstract nouns, on the other hand, are usually longer (they make up a large portion of those long words that end '-tion'). They can also be terribly vague (such as 'situation' or 'activities').

Sometimes you can replace an abstract noun with a concrete one (as in the example of 'telephone' for 'communication tool', or 'car' instead of 'transportation'). More often, though, you'll find that the best way to eliminate abstract nouns is to replace them with verbs. Here are a few examples:

- *We are suffering from bad management* can be replaced with *We are badly managed*
- *We are aiming for the elimination of faults* can be replaced with *We are aiming to eliminate faults*
- *Taking the redundancy situation into consideration . . .* can be replaced with *Considering the redundancies . . .*

Don't use pompous words or legal terms
Keep away from all those awful words like 'heretofore',
'therein', 'herewith' and so on. Nobody says them and they
can sound dreadfully pompous.

Usually you can simply remove these words without any
other change to the sentence. So *The appendix herewith
illustrates* . . . becomes *The appendix illustrates* . . . Sometimes
you may have to restructure or rephrase the sentence a
little, but it's never difficult to lose these words.

Don't use neutral words
Your report will be far easier and more interesting to read if
you inject some life into it. We've already seen how you can
do this by varying the sentence length, using active verbs,
and so on. Here's another technique.

Avoid neutral words such as 'change' when you can use an
active word such as 'improve' or 'worsen'. To give you
another example, why say *The new system affects morale*
when you could say *The new system damages morale*?

Avoid tautology
Tautology means using two or more words which mean the
same thing, rendering one of them unnecessary. 'A round
circle' is an example, or writing 'completely full' where
'full' would do.

Be careful with ambiguous words
Try saying this sentence out loud: *I'm a bit concerned about
the sales figures for the BS30 model.* You can say it in a
number of ways, and make it sound like anything from a
minor niggle to a serious problem.

That's fine if you're speaking – you can make it clear which you mean. But when you're writing, your readers don't know what you intend. What's more, the odds are they will read it one way and never realise that you could have meant something else.

Certain words can be interpreted in more than one way when written down, and you need to be careful that you make your meaning absolutely clear. Among the most common problem words to look out for are comparative words such as 'little', 'quite' and 'fairly'.

Summary

We spent today brushing up on style, in terms of your overall approach, the phrases and sentences you use, and the individual words. Once you've got into the practice of following these guidelines, your writing style will be clear and readable; qualities that will be appreciated by your readers. The main points we covered today were:

Overall style

- Use ordinary English
- Be politically correct
- Use examples and analogies

Phrasing

- Use short sentences and short paragraphs
- Don't use jargon
- Don't use clichés

Words

- Use short words
- Use active verbs
- Use concrete nouns
- Avoid pompous or legal terms
- Avoid neutral words
- Avoid tautology
- Be careful of ambiguity

Tomorrow, we'll have a look at the other aspect of writing good English: grammar. Once you've mastered both style and grammar, you'll be up there with the professional writers.

Using correct English

Yesterday we looked at how to write in a clear style. Today, we look at how to use correct English. This isn't intended to be one of those tedious and irrelevant English grammar lessons you used to have to sit through at school; we're only going to bother with the problem areas that crop up frequently:

- Vocabulary
- Spelling
- Punctuation
- Abbreviations
- Rules of grammar you can break

Anyone whose use of English is good is likely to judge you on *your* use of English. So if you want to impress your readers, you'd better brush up any problem areas you have with your grammar and spelling. It can make a big difference to the impact of your reports. So for your own sake, if you're not sure of something, don't guess – check it out.

Vocabulary

It's important to use the right word for what you're trying to say. If you don't, one or more of your readers will know you've got it wrong. For example, if you say *Some members of staff are prone to flaunt this rule . . .* someone's going to know you meant 'flout', not 'flaunt'.

Unfortunately, there's no simple rule to follow to make sure you always use the right word. But listed below are a dozen of the most commonly confused words, with a brief explanation of what they really mean. Have a look through and see if there are any that you have trouble with.

In order to explain these words, it's necessary to use a couple of grammatical terms. You probably know them anyway, but in case you had lost interest by that point in your school English lessons:

- *A verb* is a doing word
- *A noun* is a person or thing
- *An adjective* is a word that describes a noun

1 *Adverse/averse:* these are both adjectives. *Adverse* means unfavourable – *Celery has an adverse effect on me.* Averse means opposed – *I am averse to celery* (the expression used to be 'averse from' but this is now very old-fashioned).
2 *Affect/effect: affect* is a verb meaning to influence or have an impact on – *Pollution affects me badly. Effect*

can be either a verb or a noun. As a verb it means to bring about – *To effect change* – and as a noun it means an outcome – *The effect of the pollution was to make me sick.*

3 *Complement/compliment:* each of these can be either a verb or a noun. *Complement* means to complete (as a verb) or something that completes (as a noun) – *That tie complements your outfit* or *We need one more to give us a full complement. Compliment* means to praise (as a verb) or praise (as a noun) – *He complimented her* or *She paid him a compliment.*

4 *Criterion/criteria:* this one's nice and simple. *Criterion* is the singular, *criteria* is the plural. So there is *One vital criterion*, but there are *Several criteria.*

5 *Dependent/dependant: dependent* is an adjective meaning reliant – *My dog is a very dependent creature. Dependant* is a noun meaning someone who is dependent – *I have two elderly dependants.*

6 *Disk/disc:* these are both nouns, but a *disk* stores computer information while a *disc* is an object with a flat, round shape.

7 *Flaunt/flout:* these are both verbs. To *flaunt* means to show off – *He flaunted his expensive new mobile phone.* To *flout* means to show contempt for – *She flouted the rules at every opportunity.*

8 *Inquire/enquire:* these are both verbs. The first means to investigate – *The police said they would inquire into it* and the second means to ask – *She enquired after his health.*

9 *Insure/ensure:* both are verbs. To *insure* means to protect against risk – *I have insured my car.* To *ensure* means to make sure – *I want to ensure that I don't miss my train.*

10 *Mitigate/militate:* these are both verbs. To *mitigate* means to moderate or compensate – *The circumstances helped to mitigate the blame.* To *militate*, usually either 'for' or 'against', means to influence – *His words militated against her.*

11 *Practise/practice:* the first of these is a verb, the second a noun. *You need to practise if you want to get better* but *You must get plenty of practice.* You may find this one easier to learn if you remember that it follows exactly the same rule as *advise* and *advice*, or *devise* and *device.* It is harder to remember because both *practise* and *practice* are pronounced the same way. Try saying *I advise you . . .* out loud and you'll realise that the verb in each case has an *s* and the noun has a *c.*

12 *Principle/principal:* the first is a noun and means a standard – *It's against his principles.* The second can be a noun or an adjective, meaning the primary or most important – *The principal of the college* or *The principal question we need to answer.*

Finally, it can't be emphasised too strongly that if you're not sure, you should look the word up. At the end of this chapter you'll find a list of the most useful books to keep on your bookshelf which, between them, should cover everything you could ever want to know about how to use the English language correctly.

Spelling

Once again, getting this wrong gives a bad impression, so always check if you're not sure. You may have a spell check on your computer; if so, use it with caution or not at all.

The danger with spell checks is that people tend to rely on them and do no other checking. But spell checks miss anything that is a real word, even if it's not the one you intended. So if you want to type 'too' meaning also, and you leave off the final 'o', the spell check won't pick it up; 'to' is still a word after all. It's just not the one you meant.

The best system with spell checks is to make yourself a rule that you will use them only if you also do a thorough check yourself. They will save you time looking up a few words in the dictionary. If your spelling is dreadful, and especially for an important report, ask someone else to check it through for you as well.

Here are a few words that are commonly misspelt and worth making a particular note of (or remember that they are here and come back to this page to look them up when you use them):

* Accommodate
* Commitment
* Enrol
* Gauge
* Mileage
* Privilege
* Appal
* Embarrass
* Fulfil
* Harass
* Parallel
* Questionnaire

English is a particularly difficult language to spell in – much more difficult than, say, Italian. English has very few regular formulas to follow, and many words are not spelt anything like they sound. There are a few guidelines, however, to help you with at least some groups of words:

1 Many words are obviously made up of a common word plus a prefix (a bit that goes in front). If you break the word down into these two separate components it's easier to tell

whether there should be a double letter in the middle. Take 'misspelt' as an example. This has a double 's' in the middle because you have merged the two parts 'mis' and 'spelt' and kept the 's' from each. This also happens with 'unnecessary' which is made up of 'un' and 'neces-sary'. However, 'uneven' has only one 'n' in the middle, because you have merged 'un' and 'even'.

2 The Americans end words in '-ize' which we end in '-ise', such as realize/realise or organize/organise. If you think your readers would prefer the English version, use the '-ise' ending for these words.

3 'Benefited' has one 't' in the middle and 'regretted' has two. Believe it or not, there's a reason for this. If the stress is on the last syllable of the word you double the final letter when you add '-ed'. So 'reg*ret*' becomes 'regretted'. If the stress falls earlier in the word ('*ben*efit') you leave the single letter at the end: 'benefited'.
This rule also explains the single letters at the end of 'marketed', 'focused' and 'targeted' – all commonly misspelt. There is one exception to this rule which is when the final letter is an 'l'. This is always doubled, as in 'travelled'.

4 If you are putting '-ly' on the end of a word which already ends in 'l' (such as full/fully), it always becomes a double 'll', regardless of whether the original word had one or two 'l's at the end of it. So 'wool' becomes 'woolly', 'special' becomes 'specially', 'dull' becomes 'dully', 'final' becomes 'finally' and so on.

5 Remember the rule '*i* before *e* except after *c*'. There are very few exceptions to this. The only notable ones are:
• The word 'seize'
• Some place names and personal names

- Words in which the *ei* is not pronounced 'eee', such as inveigle

Punctuation

There are certain points of punctuation that can be quite difficult to get to grips with. We'll take a look at the main ones:

- Apostrophes
- Colons
- Semi-colons
- Hyphens
- Exclamation marks
- Capital letters

Apostrophes
The biggest mistake people make with apostrophes is to use them to make a word plural (such as potato's, 1990's and so on). There is no word in the English language that

requires an apostrophe for this: it is *always* wrong to do it. An apostrophe has two functions:

- To show that a letter has been missed out
- To indicate possession

Missing out a letter

You need to use an apostrophe if you elide two words, to show where letters have been missed. Examples of this include 'isn't', 'wouldn't', 'can't' and so on.

'It's' has an apostrophe if it is short for 'it is', and never for any other reason. If you're not sure whether to include an apostrophe in 'its' just say the sentence in your head, replacing 'its' with 'it is'. If it makes sense, use the apostrophe; otherwise don't. Here are a couple of examples:

- *I'll miss the train unless it's late.* This makes sense as . . . *unless it is late* so it needs an apostrophe
- *Is this your dog? What's its name?* If you say this to yourself as *What's it is name?* the sentence is meaningless. So it isn't short for 'it is' and therefore shouldn't have an apostrophe

Possession

If something belongs to the manager, the desk, the department or whatever, you can add an 's' to the end of the word: the manager's office, the desk's bottom drawer, the department's budget. So far, so good.

The apostrophe goes after whoever (or whatever) is doing the possessing. So if the owners are plural the apostrophe goes after the 's'. *The manager's office* indicates that there is one manager. If several of them share an office you would write *The managers' office.* The easiest way to remember it is to say to yourself *the . . . belonging to the . . .* If it's the office belonging to the managers, the apostrophe goes after the 's'.

You may have spotted that this rule leaves room for confusion if the word in question happens to end in an 's'. In this case you simply put the apostrophe at the end of the word (e.g. *the census'*). There are two exceptions to this: if it's a proper name (e.g. *Mr. Thomas's*) or if the word ends in a double 's' (e.g. *the boss's*).

Possessive pronouns (these are the words like 'yours', 'ours', 'hers', 'its', 'theirs') never have apostrophes.

Colons
Colons are there to signpost the next piece of text; however, they should be used only to indicate the totality of what went before. So you can say *There is only one rule: there are no rules.*

But you shouldn't use a colon to indicate an incomplete list, only a complete one. For example, *Here are the ingredients of a sponge cake: sugar, butter, eggs, flour and a little milk* is a complete list. An incomplete list should simply be signalled by words such as 'including' or 'like'. For example, *The ingredients of a sponge cake include sugar, butter and eggs.*

Colons break the flow of the sentence, so don't use one if the sentence works without it. For example, *The ingredients of a sponge cake are sugar, butter, eggs, flour and a little milk.* Some people would be tempted (wrongly) to add a colon after the word 'are'.

Semi-colons
There are two reasons for using a semi-colon:

- To give a strong break but one that is not quite as strong as a full stop
- To break up a list that already contains commas

There are times when you want more than a comma but less than a full stop; this is where semi-colons are most often used.

The best way to break up a list is with commas, because the reader's eyes flow more smoothly through commas than semi-colons. However, sometimes one or more of the items in the list already contain commas. This is when you should use semi-colons to separate the items: *Food products such as nuts; eggs; flour; milk, butter and cheese; rice . . .*

Hyphens
The point of a hyphen is to make the sense clearer; to show that two words are closely linked. But hyphens make the text visually harder to read, which reduces the clarity. So you should use a hyphen if the dictionary states that a word is hyphenated, or if you think the sentence is really unclear without it. But if in doubt, leave it out.

Exclamation marks
There's just one rule about exclamation marks: never use them at the end of a sentence to tell the reader it was supposed to be funny. Exclamation marks are for exclamations, and nothing else.

Capital letters
Capital letters are harder to read than lower case letters, so don't use them unless you have to. For example, don't write *Managing Director – managing director* is far better.

Abbreviations

If you shorten words in a report it implies that the reader wasn't worth bothering to write the word out for in full. So avoid abbreviations such as 'approx' (you can always replace it with 'about' if you don't want to bother to write it out in full). Another one to avoid for the same reason is 'etc.', which can be replaced with a phrase such as 'and so on'.

Abbreviating long titles to their initials, however, makes the text much easier to read. There's nothing worse than a piece of writing which is largely made up of lengthy names of organisations and so on. But the reader does need to know what the initials stand for.

The rule for overcoming this is simple. The first time you refer to the organisation, product or whatever it is, you give the title in full immediately followed by the initials in brackets. For example: *The Department of Social Security (DSS).* After that, you can simply refer to it as *the DSS.*

The MD and the CEO have asked the R&D Dept to bring forward the e.t.a. for the XP30 launch to 1st Jan.

Rules of grammar you can break

This is the fun bit, if there's a rebel lurking in you anywhere. If you talk to anyone who was educated in the 1960s or earlier – or if you were yourself – you have probably been told all sorts of rules of grammar. The good news is that several of these rules are now out of date, and you no longer have to follow them. Of course, if you are writing for old-fashioned readers you'd better not flout the rules, but for any other readership, here are the main rules that you now have permission to break.

1 *Never begin a sentence with 'and' or 'but'.* This rule was only invented because people wanted to do it in the first place. Why did they want to? Because it's a very useful device for adding emphasis to the 'and' or 'but'. So go ahead and do it if it seems appropriate. What's more, you can start paragraphs with these words as well, if you like.

2 *Never finish a sentence with a preposition.* Prepositions are all those little words that aren't nouns or verbs or anything else. Words like 'of', 'with', 'up' and so on. Feel free to put them anywhere you like. Winston Churchill is supposed to have thought this particular rule of grammar ludicrous, and demonstrated his opinion – when his secretary ticked him off for breaking the rule – by saying 'There are some things up with which I will not put!'

3 *Never split an infinitive.* These days, it's rare to find someone who can confidently identify a split infinitive, let alone cares whether it is split or not. If you don't know whether you're splitting your infinitives or not, don't worry about it.

Summary

We spent today looking at how to use correct English. All those niggly little rules that matter to some of your readers, and therefore have to matter to you.

We started by looking at vocabulary and spelling, and listed some of the most commonly misused or misspelt words. We also looked at a few general rules for spelling. After that, we checked out the most common problem areas with punctuation, and then brushed up on when and how to use abbreviations. Finally, we established three rules you're allowed to break if you want to.

Don't forget that many readers whose mastery of English is good will judge you by *your* use of English, among other things. If you want to impress them, earn their respect and retain credibility in their eyes, you will have to learn to write to their standards.

For this reason, you should never guess at any point of English usage. If you're not sure of something – spelling, the meaning of a word, where to put an apostrophe or anything else – look it up.

There are four books that anyone who writes reports with any frequency should keep on their bookshelf. Between them, they will tell you everything that is worth knowing about the English language:

1 *Dictionary.* Get the best dictionary you can, and be prepared to replace it every ten years or so. New words get added and some words change their usage.
2 *Thesaurus. Roget's Thesaurus* is the classic one, and probably still the best. If you can't quite think of the word

you want, you can look up a similar word in the index of the thesaurus. The index will direct you to a list of synonyms – words with the same or very similar meaning. Invariably you will find the word you were trying to remember, along with plenty more.

3 *The Complete Plain Words* by Sir Ernest Gowers. This is one of the best books you will find on any subject. It has been, for the last 40 years, the definitive guide to writing good, plain English. It's also a damn good read, packed with useful and entertaining examples. It is as useful as a dictionary or a thesaurus.

4 *Fowler's Modern English Usage* (Oxford University Press). This book was first published 70 years ago, and has since been revised and updated. The edition currently in print was edited by Dr Robert Burchfield and is a modern guide to anything you could possibly need to know about English grammar and usage, from metaphors and similes to punctuation and participles. It will even tell you what a split infinitive is.

Adding the finishing touches

We're nearly there. We've done all the preparation and structuring, and written the report. Now it's just a matter of adding the finishing touches:

- Layout
- Appendices
- Using charts and graphs
- Any extras

If you had guests for dinner whom you wanted to impress, you would make sure that the food you served up was well-presented and looked appetising. In the same way, if you want to impress people with your reports, you need to ensure that they, too, are well-presented and look attractive and readable.

YOUR REPORT, SIR

Layout

As we all know, first impressions are vital. And the first thing your readers will notice when they pick up your report – before they read a word of it – is the way it looks.

You know yourself that if you look at a book, magazine article or report you make instinctive judgements based on the layout of the text. You decide that it looks fun, impenetrable, manageable, heavy going, easy to read or whatever. Your readers will do the same with your report, so you need to make sure that it gives the best possible impression.

The aim is twofold: firstly, you want to make the report look readable; and secondly, you want to make it look organised. Your readers will associate you personally with the qualities they attribute to your report. So if you want them to see you as organised, professional and authoritative, you need to give your report these qualities. The layout is a big part of that.

There are several aspects of the layout that will help to make your report look more readable, so we'll look at each of them in turn.

Spacing and margins
The more space there is around your text, the more approachable and manageable it will seem. So double space it, and leave fairly wide margins. Wide margins have the added advantage of focusing attention on the text, which makes it look more important.

You'll need to consider whether or not to justify the right hand margin – in other words to line up the right hand ends of all the lines. It all depends on the impression you want to give.

Unjustified text
Unjustified text looks friendlier and more informal. This can be a benefit if the report is quite informal, or if the readers could be put off by it.

For example, if you're writing a report on a highly technical subject for non-technical readers, you might want to do everything you can to make them feel that they will be able to understand the technical bits, and that the report isn't going to be over their heads. In this case, you may well feel that it would be a good idea to leave the text unjustified.

Justified text
Justified text looks more formal, which can be an advantage with some reports. Its other benefit is that it looks slightly tidier. Normally this doesn't make a significant difference, but sometimes a report can run the risk of looking rather confusing if there are lots of diagrams or charts in it. In this case, justifying the right hand margin will help to keep it looking neat and tidy.

Whether or not you decide to justify the right hand margin, you should stick to your decision all the way through the report.

Headings
Headings have three useful functions.

- Firstly, they break the page up and make it look more readable

- Secondly, headings tell the reader what is coming next; they help to signpost the report. For some people, this gives a clear overview of where the sense of the report is heading. For others, it tells them that this is a bit they can afford to skip if they are pushed for time
- Thirdly, headings are really useful if the reader wants to refer back to something later on – they can find it far more easily

So it's important for headings to indicate clearly what the next bit of text is about. Don't try to dream up clever or witty headings. They may be great in a newspaper, but they're no good for reports.

Sections
As well as giving each section a fresh heading or subheading, you may also want to number the sections. This gives a slightly more formal appearance – once again, you will need to decide whether this is what you want.

Numbering sections is mostly helpful so that people can discuss the report with each other, or with you, later. It makes it easier for them to direct each other to the part of the report they are referring to. There's not much point in doing it if this isn't going to happen. If it is, there are several ways of numbering sections:

1 You can give a number to each headed section, for example, *3 Benefits to customers.*
2 You can number each new paragraph below the headings.
3 You can combine these two approaches by numbering each heading, and then giving each paragraph within it a

number as well. So your sequence will go: 1.1, 1.2, 1.3
and so on. It's not worth trying to break the numbers
down beyond this (1.1.1, 1.1.2, 1.1.3 . . . .) as this is
simply confusing.

Lists

Lists are always easier to follow than the same information
presented as solid text, so use them when you can. You
might be listing benefits, disadvantages, techniques you
used to gather information – always use a list if you think it
might help. It also makes the page easier to read and take in.

You can use various devices to indicate lists, such as bullet
points, numbers and so on. You may even have a suitable
icon on your word processor. If you're writing a report on
upgrading the telephone system, for example, you could
signal each new point on the list with a little icon of a
phone. Don't get too clever though, or keep switching
icons, as this distracts from what you're saying.

General design

Finally, keep your design clean and simple, to avoid
distracting from the content. You don't need more than two
typefaces – one for text and one for headings. And keep
your style of headings simple and consistent.

Appendices

How do you feel when a 60-page report lands on your desk
and you're expected to read the whole thing? Or even a
20-page report? People don't like long reports, and they
often have difficulty finding time to read them. So keep
your report as short as possible.

You should be able to get just about any report down to under ten pages (of course there will be a few exceptions, for major research projects). If your report is only three pages long people won't think you're lazy; they'll be grateful to you – assuming it tells them what they want to know. Your readers want quality, not quantity.

But suppose you've got 30 pages worth of information that readers might want? That's what the appendices are for. Give them the bare facts in the main body of the report. When it comes to proving the facts, or showing how you arrived at them, simply direct readers to the appendix. Then they can read it or not as they want to.

Once you have taken out this kind of information and put it at the back, you should have no trouble keeping your report nice and brief. You can include the following in an appendix:

- Statistics
- Graphs and charts
- Sets of figures
- Information you may want to update during the life-time of the report
- Methodology
- Copies of survey forms and other research data

Charts and graphs

Very often, the best way for the reader to take in information is in the form of graphs or charts, rather than tables of figures. Not only are they faster to read but, more importantly, you can also use them to draw attention to the aspect of the data you want to emphasise most strongly.

But how exactly do you do that? And which kind of chart or graph should you use when? In fact, they all have different functions. Depending on what you are trying to illustrate, there is only one kind of diagram that will do the job properly. So let's look at the main types of graph and chart, and see what you should use each one for.

All charts and graphs are used to show comparisons between things. So to begin with, we need to establish what you might be trying to compare. There are five main types of comparison you are likely to need to illustrate.

Components
If you are breaking a single figure or item into parts, and showing how it is divided, you are making a component comparison. For example, you could be demonstrating the total number of employees in the organisation, and illustrating how many are employed in each department.

Where you are adding up components that total 100%, you should use a pie chart. This shouldn't have more than about half a dozen sections, or it will be too confusing to take in.

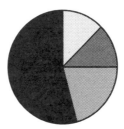

You shouldn't use two pie charts next to each other to compare, say, share of departmental spend on stationery with share of spend on mileage. It's just too difficult for the reader's eye to pull out the relevant information. For this kind of component comparison, use two 100% bar charts next to each other. A 100% bar chart shows the same thing as a pie chart.

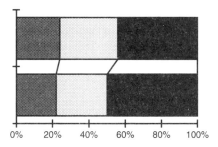

Items

If you want to compare one item with another, you need to use a bar chart. For example, you might want to show how many employees there are in the company, but with a different emphasis. If you're not emphasising the total and how it was made up, but you want to emphasise the difference between the number of employees in each department (the departments being the items you're comparing), this is the way to do it.

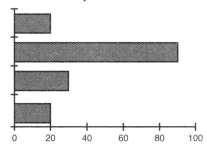

Many people use column charts for this (we're about to look at them), but the problem with a column chart is that it implies a time scale – from left to right – which doesn't exist in this case. So it's better to use a horizontal chart.

Time series

If you want to indicate a trend over time, such as how

numbers have changed over the last few years, you need to
use a column chart or a line chart. A column chart is the
vertical equivalent of a bar chart.

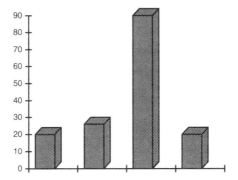

A line chart is better if you are marking a lot of time points
– for example the change in employee numbers over the
last 24 months. Also, a column chart draws attention to the
change between each month's figures, while a line chart
puts more emphasis on the overall trend.

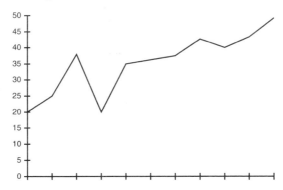

Frequency distribution
This is something you often want to demonstrate when
giving the results of surveys. In this case you are
comparing how many items fall into each of several

numerical ranges. These might be 'under 18 years old', '19–25', '26–35' and so on. Or it might be 'under £20', '£20–£50'. . . If you want to show a frequency distribution, you need to use a column chart (which we've already seen).

Correlation
You can show whether the number of employees in each department correlates with the departmental budget, by using two bar charts back to back.

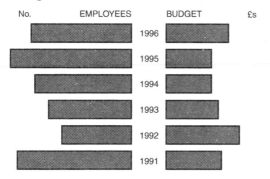

Any extras

If you look at any book (including this one) you'll find it has a title page, information about copyright, a contents list and so on. Your reports should supply the same – or at least the equivalent.

There are some features which you should include in virtually every report, as standard, and others that will apply only sometimes.

Regular features
You may have a house style for writing reports which you are expected to follow. Assuming you are free to include what you choose, several features should appear in just about

every report, whatever the length (the only common exception to this is a memo, which is a kind of short report):

- Title page
- Author's name – on the title page
- Date of report – also on the title page, often in the bottom right hand corner unless it's integral to the report (such as a monthly update) in which case it should have more prominence
- Contents page
- The objective – at the start of the report
- A summary (we'll cover this later)
- An appendix or appendices – at the back, but clearly signposted in the relevant part of the report
- Page numbers

Occasional extras

Sometimes, there are other features that your readers will also find useful. The extras listed below should all go at the back of the report, and should be indicated on the contents page:

- A glossary – if you have been unable to avoid including jargon
- A bibliography
- References to your sources (the ones we looked at on Monday) – this will add to your credibility, and you can point to them if anyone challenges your authority
- Useful addresses
- Acknowledgements – if other people have helped with the report or contributed to it

The summary

This is the very last thing you need to write. You might think that you would start by writing the summary – particularly since it will go at the front of the report – but in fact it's far easier to write it after you've done everything else. Then you know precisely what it is that you're summarising.

Unless your report is extremely short – fewer than three or four pages - it should always have a summary at the beginning. The summary is useful for:

- People who just won't have time to read the full report
- Those who do read the whole report but who may want to remind themselves later without reading it all again

You can see from this that the summary needs to say everything that the whole report says – only more briefly. It's not a conclusion but a précis.

So when it comes to structuring your summary, it should follow the same structure as the full report. State the aim or objective, and then summarise your methods, results and conclusion.

The summary must never run over a page, or you start to defeat the point of writing it in the first place. However, for a report of only four or five pages you may well find that your summary is only a couple of paragraphs. That's fine; it's precisely what your readers want.

Summary

We spent today putting the finishing touches to the report – the icing on the cake. If you want to make a good first impression on your readers, you need the report to look attractive and readable at first glance. We've looked at how to use the layout to create the right effect.

We also looked at how to keep the report nice and brief for busy readers by putting any supplementary information into an appendix. This includes any figures, graphs, tables, survey forms and so on that back up the main body of the report.

Charts and graphs can go in the main report or the appendices. Either way, it can be tricky converting information into chart or graph form if you don't know which type of chart to use. So we looked at choosing the right chart to suit the information you're trying to put across.

Finally, we had a quick look at all the extra features that you will – or may – need to add to your report, from the title page to 'useful addresses'. And we looked at how to write a brief summary to go at the front of the report, if it runs beyond three or four pages.

Tomorrow we'll spend the day recapping everything we covered this week. By the time we've finished that, you'll know everything you need to know to turn out top class reports.

Checklist of key points

We've spent the last week studying the skills and techniques of report writing. That's exactly what they are – techniques – anyone can learn them. They don't require any inborn talent.

The six stages of report writing which we covered in the last week, and which we recap today, are:

- Setting the objective
- Researching and organising the information
- Structuring the report
- Writing in a clear style
- Using correct English
- Adding the finishing touches

You have now learnt one of the really central management skills, and one that many managers never really learn at all. This has a number of benefits for you personally:

1 You should start to find that your written recommendations get accepted more often. That's one of the effects of well written reports. People take them – and the conclusions they incorporate – more seriously

2 Even your regular reports, updates and memos will reflect well on you. Both your bosses and your own team will judge you by the written material you produce, and they will start to see you as efficient, organised and clear thinking – a pretty good reputation to have

3 If you're in a large organisation, it's only a matter of time before someone further up the organisation notices you because of a particularly well put together report. It's surprising how many successful managers can date one or more of their crucial steps up the career ladder to a particularly impressive report they wrote that caught the eye of someone influential.

You'll probably find you have to work quite hard at report writing to begin with, but you should already be able to turn out top class reports. Once you've had a bit more practice you'll find it gets easier and easier.

But the chances are that you'll still want to refer back to this book for quite a while, just to be sure you're on the right track until your confidence has built up thoroughly.

So this chapter is a checklist of key points from each of the earlier chapters.

Setting the objective

We started on Sunday by taking a look at the very first step in writing reports: setting the objective. We looked at why you need an objective, and then at the three steps in setting the objective:

Why you need an objective

- It helps you decide what information to include or omit
- It helps you pitch the report appropriately for the reader
- It makes it easier to write the report

How to set the objective

To do this, you need to ask yourself a series of questions:

- Who is going to read the report?
- Why do they want it?
- What aspects do they want to know about?
- What do they *not* want to know?
- How much do they know about the subject?

Making the objective specific

Establish the requirements of the report, and build them into the objective to make it more specific.

Agreeing the objective

Once you've written down the objective, show it to
your boss or whoever asked for the report. Get them
to agree that the report you think you are writing is the
one they think they asked for.

Researching and organising the information

We spent Monday looking at the second stage of report
writing: researching and organising the information. There
were four steps to this part of the process:

Decide what information you need

- Refer to your objective and draw up a list of general
  topics
- Write these down in any random order for now
- List subtopics under these general headings

Collect the material

There are three main sources you can go to for
information:

- Material from inside your organisation (e.g. sales
  brochures, newsletters, regular reports, minutes of
  meetings, other people's reports)
- Publicly available material (from books, directories,
  the press, trade associations, government departments, competitors)
- Information you get from talking to people (customers, experts, suppliers)

Collate the information

Write a summary of each point you want to include on a separate slip of paper, with a note of where to find the information in full

Sort it into groups

Organise these slips of paper into logical groups, usually between four and a dozen of them. At this stage, the groups you put the information into needn't relate to the final structure of the report

Structuring the report

On Tuesday we finished the preparation stages by looking at how to structure the report. There are two different types of report when it comes to structuring: research reports and information-only reports.

Research reports

In a research report, you study a subject and then report on your findings. This may or may not include recommendations on how to use the findings.

The structure of a research report is the same as the structure you use to write up a scientific experiment: aim, method, results, conclusion.

Aim

This is the objective you worked out on Sunday, and is expressed as a single sentence. A research report would normally include this at the beginning.

Method

In this part of the report, you explain how you went about researching the subject, and the sources you used (in brief; you don't want to include a detailed bibliography or interview list). If you conducted any experiments, surveys, tests or anything of that kind, you need to explain briefly what your approach was.

Results

This is where you present your findings, but you need to make sure that at this stage you remain as neutral and objective as possible. Just give them the facts. Avoid getting bogged down in unnecessary detail – save that for the appendix if it needs to be included anywhere, and simply direct the reader to it.

Conclusion

This is the final section, in which you can express any subjective view drawn from the results of your research, or any recommendations if you have been asked to include these in your report. The conclusion should not normally run over a page, except in the biggest of research projects.

Information-only reports

Structuring an information-only report is simply a matter of organising the groups of information you already have into the most logical order. This may be by date, turnover, location, order of importance or whatever. Just occasionally there may be no obvious sequence at all, in which case don't worry about the order. You can't create logic where it simply doesn't exist.

Remember that the structure is there to help the reader to:

- Follow the information easily
- Take in the information and understand it
- Go back later and find any information quickly if they want to recap

Writing in a clear style

Wednesday was all about your style of writing, and how to make it suitable and clear for your readers. We looked at overall style, phrasing and words.

Overall style
The important thing is to make the style suitable for your readers; after all, you're writing the report for them, not yourself. Your own natural style is likely to be appropriate for most of your readers, but there are some people for whom you may need to adapt your usual style:

- People with a more traditional style of English
- People with a more modern style than yours
- People for whom English is not the first language
- People with dyslexia or other reading difficulties

Use ordinary English
Stick to everyday language when you write – you should write pretty much as you speak, apart from avoiding slang and extreme colloquialisms. For example:

- Elide words where it seems natural, such as 'it's' for 'it is'

- Avoid stilted language
- Refer to yourself as 'I', or 'we' if you are writing on behalf of a group or department
- Address the reader as 'you'

Be politically correct

It is your readers' views on this that count, not yours. Even if your readers don't find it offensive, they are increasingly likely to find it outdated. But if you use non-sexist, non-racist, non-ageist language carefully, no one will even notice that you're doing it. There are a few useful techniques for avoiding sexist language:

- Put the sentence into the plural
- Use the second person ('you' or 'your')
- Use 'they' as a singular
- If you're giving examples of types of people, alternate examples of men and women
- Use 'he or she' or 'he/she' (but bear in mind that the other options are preferable)

Use examples and analogies

Your readers can't interrupt and ask you to repeat something that they don't understand, as they could if you were talking to them. So you need to be sure that they understand what you're saying first time.

If there's any chance that your readers might need an example, give them one. It never hurts to give examples, so play it safe and supply plenty of them.

If you have a complicated idea to explain, use an analogy. Tell the reader that 'it's a bit like . . .' or 'it's as if . . .'

Phrasing

Overall style may be crucial, but it isn't the whole story. We looked at how you can make the phrasing as clear and understandable as possible for your readers:

- Use short sentences – average about 20 words and don't go over 40 words
- Keep paragraphs short – on an A4 page they should be wider than they are deep
- Don't use jargon – an everyday word to you may be jargon to your readers
- Don't use clichés – give hard facts instead

Words

We also looked at the individual words you use:

- Use short words when you can
- Use active rather than passive verbs – have the subject of the sentence do something, rather than have something done to them
- Use concrete rather than abstract nouns – 'car' rather than 'transportation'
- Don't use pompous or legal terms such as 'hereinafter'
- Don't use neutral words – say 'improve' rather than 'change'
- Avoid tautology – two words meaning the same thing, such as 'round circle'
- Be careful with ambiguous words – such as 'quite'

Using correct English

Having dealt with how to write in a clear style on Wednesday, on Thursday we looked at how to use correct English. We covered the most common problem areas in vocabulary, spelling, punctuation and abbreviations. Then we checked out some old fashioned rules of grammar that it's OK to break these days, and finished with a brief list of the books you really should have on your shelf.

Vocabulary
We established that it's very important to use the right word for what you're trying to say. If you misuse a word and your readers know you've got it wrong, their opinion of you and your report is almost guaranteed to go down. You may feel this is unfair – but that's the way it is. So if you're in any doubt at all about the correct use of a word, look it up. Don't take a chance.

We then went through a dozen of the most commonly confused words, and explained the distinction between them.

Spelling
As with vocabulary, we established the importance of checking if you're not certain how a word is spelt. Computer spell checks are unreliable, so always ask someone else whose grammar and spelling are good to look through an important report for you. Although English spelling is irritatingly unpredictable, we did identify a few useful rules of spelling.

Punctuation
We had a look at the main problem areas with punctuation, and summarised the rules.

Apostrophes

An apostrophe should never be used to pluralise a word. It has only two functions:

- To show that a letter has been missed out
- To indicate possession

Colons

Colons are there to signpost the next piece of text. When used to indicate a list, they should signpost only a complete list to follow.

Since it breaks the flow of the text, you shouldn't use a colon if the sentence works just as well without it.

Semi-colons

There are only two reasons for using a semi-colon:

- To give a break that is more than a comma but less than a full stop
- To break up a list that already contains commas

Hyphens

You should use a hyphen if the dictionary tells you that a word is hyphenated, or if the meaning would be unclear without it. Since hyphens make the text harder to read, you should not use them if neither of these two conditions applies.

Exclamation marks

Exclamation marks don't exist to tell the reader that the last sentence was supposed to be funny. They should be used for exclamations and nothing else.

Capital letters

Like hyphens, capital letters are harder to read. So use them where you must – chiefly the beginning of sentences and proper names – but avoid them otherwise.

Abbreviations

We also looked at how to use abbreviations. We established that you shouldn't use shortened words such as 'approx' and 'etc.' because it is insulting to the reader not to bother to write the word out in full.

However, you should use initials instead of long titles if you can. Use the full name or title the first time you mention it, immediately followed by the initials in brackets. After that, simply use the initials each time.

Adding the finishing touches

We spent Friday looking at the final stage of report writing; topping and tailing. We looked at the main points of layout, appendices, charts and graphs and any extras.

Layout

- Double space your text, and leave fairly wide margins
- Use plenty of headings and subheadings
- Number sections if you think this will help the reader
- Use lists rather than continuous text where you can
- Keep the design clean and simple

Appendices

Use an appendix for any supplementary information, to keep the main body of the report brief

Charts and graphs

- For component comparison use a pie chart. To compare two groups of components use two 100% bar charts
- For item comparison use a bar chart
- For time series comparison use a column chart or a line chart
- For frequency distribution comparison use a column chart
- For correlation use two bar charts back to back

Any extras

- Include regular features such as the title page
- Consider occasional extras such as a glossary
- Always add a summary except for the shortest of reports

For information

on other

IN A WEEK titles

go to

www.inaweek.co.uk